EDGE
BOOKS™

NATURE'S
INVADERS

INFESTATION!

ROACHES, BEDBUGS, ANTS,
AND OTHER INSECT INVADERS

BY SHARON L. REITH

Consultant:
Michael Bright, Chartered Biologist (CBiol)
BBC wildlife filmmaker
United Kingdom

CAPSTONE PRESS
a capstone imprint

Edge Books are published by Capstone Press,
1710 Roe Crest Drive, North Mankato, Minnesota 56003
www.capstonepub.com

Library of Congress Cataloging-in-Publication Data
Reith, Sharon L., author.
 Infestation! / by Sharon L. Reith.
   pages cm. — (Edge books. Nature's invaders)
 Summary: "A look at insect species that infest homes and other buildings and what
can be done to prevent unwanted visitors from invading your home"—Provided by
publisher.
 Audience: 3 to 9.
 Audience: Grades 4 to 6.
 Includes bibliographical references and index.
 ISBN 978-1-4765-0139-0 (library binding)
1. Insects--Juvenile literature. 2. Household pests--Juvenile literature. 3. Insects as
carriers of disease--Juvenile literature. I. Title.
 QL467.2.R456 2014
 595.7165--dc23

                    2013019588

Editorial Credits
Adrian Vigliano, editor; Ted Williams, designer; Eric Manske, production specialist

Photo Credits
BigStockPhoto.com/Scott Harms, 1, 3 (ants), 5; CDC, 14-15 (both), Piotr Naskrecki,
cover (bedbug); Corbis: Visuals Unlimited/Alex Wild, 28, ZUMA Press/The Toronto
Star/Andrew Wallace, 25; Dreamstime: Fechetm, 13; iStockphotos: BanksPhotos,
3 (spraying), jmalov, 16-17, Lynn Bunting, 3 (stink bug); National Geographic
Stock: George Grall, 27, Minden Pictures/Mark Moffett, cover, 12 (ants); Newscom:
ZUMAPress/The Toronto Star/David Cooper, 21; Science Source: Pascal Goetgheluck,
7; Shutterstock: Andre Maritz, 3 (cockroach), Dmitri Gomon, 7 (inset), ex0rzist, 10
(inset), gosphotodesign, cover (cockroaches), jareynolds, 3 (bedbug), Paula Cobleigh,
9, Smit, 19; USDA, 10; Wikimedia/Charlysays, 20-21, Thmazing, 22-23

Design Elements
Shutterstock: dcwcreations, foxie, happykanppy, JohnySima, jumpingsack, Michal
Ninger, sdecoret

Printed in the United States of America in Stevens Point, Wisconsin.
032013   007227WZF13

TABLE OF CONTENTS

CHAPTER ONE

INFESTED!

The Junod family had a problem. There were so many ants in their house that the floor looked like it was moving. Ants crawled in the bathtub and over their food. They had an Argentine ant **infestation**.

Insects such as ants, cockroaches, and bedbugs are some of the toughest insect invaders. Once they move in, they are extremely hard to get rid of.

WHY DID THIS HAPPEN?

Insect invaders are in search of three things: food, water, and shelter. If insects find these in your home, they will stay as long as they can.

Insects reproduce quickly. A queen ant's job is to lay eggs. She can lay up to 1,000 eggs each day. Cockroaches live from a few months to about two years. But during that time, the females can lay many eggs. One female cockroach can lay 300 to 400 eggs in her lifetime. Just one female bedbug can lay as many as 200 eggs in her lifetime, which may last from around six months to several years.

⚠ FOREIGN INVADER

The Argentine ant arrived in New Orleans, Louisiana, in the 1890s on a coffee ship. Since then, it has spread across the southern and western United States. These aggressive ants attack and destroy other ant colonies, wasp nests, and bird nests. Argentine ants are especially good at working together to keep their colony strong. If the queen dies, a new queen will take over and the colony will survive.

• Argentine ants swarm outside of their colony.

✗ infestation—a group of pests that can cause damage or harm

FINDING A NEW WAY TO SURVIVE

Cockroach-like creatures have been around for 350 million years and ants for 120 million years. **Fossils** of hundreds of ant and cockroach **species** have been found. Before people existed, these ancient insects ate mainly decaying plants and animals. Some of them became the pests we know today by living in caves with early humans. They began to live off of people's water, food, and shelter. Fossils of bedbugs that are 3,500 years old have also been found. Bedbugs started to live off the blood of early humans instead of living off the blood of animals.

Invaders Fact

Scientists believe that cockroaches have **adapted** so well that they could survive the radiation from a nuclear bomb.

* **fossil**—the remains or traces of plants and animals that are preserved as rock

* **species**—a group of plants or animals that share common characteristics

* **adapt**—to change to fit into a new or different environment

ALL ABOARD!

Imagine sailing on a ship infested with cockroaches. Sir Francis Drake, an English sea captain, once captured a ship just like that. The ship, named *San Felipe*, was captured in 1587. In the 1780s, Captain William Bligh recorded in his logs that boiling water killed the cockroaches onboard his infested ship, *Bounty*.

● This cockroach fossil is between 161 and 176 million years old.

COCKROACH

Location: worldwide, except polar regions

Why a problem? cockroaches carry over 50 dangerous diseases

Key points:

❏ thirty of more than 4,000 species are pests to humans

❏ commonly infest apartments and hotel or restaurant kitchens

❏ just one female cockroach can lead to a huge infestation

CHAPTER TWO

KNOW YOUR INSECT INVADERS

People have been trying to keep insects out of their homes for hundreds of years. The first pest control company was formed in 1695. This company, Tiffin & Son of London, England, killed bedbugs for the country's royalty. Early **exterminators** knew it was important to learn about the insects they were trying to kill. Today scientists know more than ever about insects. Exterminators can use the information scientists have gathered to help them do their jobs.

DISEASE CARRIERS

Cockroaches are originally from Asia and Northern Africa. They first traveled to the United States long ago aboard wooden sailing ships. People have been trying to get rid of cockroaches for hundreds of years because they carry dangerous diseases.

Cockroaches will eat almost anything, even trash, sewage, and glue. When cockroaches eat, they throw up some of their food, leaving little bits of their meal behind. They also poop as they eat and crawl along, spreading bacteria in the process. Cockroaches are known to carry at least 50 different disease-causing bacteria. Substances in their poop and saliva can also cause people to itch, sneeze, or cough.

✗ **exterminator**—a person who rids places of unwanted pests for a living

● Cockroaches have wings, but usually skitter along walls and through cracks.

● Stinkbugs suck juices from fruits and vegetables, leaving dark brown spots.

BROWN MARMORATED STINKBUG

Location: originally from China, Korea, and Japan; currently spreading across North America

Why a problem? destroys fruit and vegetable crops; produces bad odor and buzzing sounds

Key points:

❑ causes serious damage to fruit and vegetable crops

❑ has no natural predators in North America

❑ bad odor smells like the herb cilantro

NEW ARRIVAL

One of the newest insect invaders to the United States is the brown **marmorated** stinkbug. Scientists think it came from Asia to North America on a ship. The brown marmorated stinkbug was first recorded in Pennsylvania in 1998. Since then this species has spread across the country, even reaching California. It has invaded 38 states, and it's still on the move.

SMELLY GUESTS

As the weather gets cooler, stinkbugs begin looking for indoor warmth. Once they are in a house, they may get into laundry, climb walls, and even end up in your lunch box! These are all signs of a stinkbug infestation.

Brown marmorated stinkbugs cause major damage to crops, but inside homes, they are basically harmless. They do not sting, bite, or cause damage to houses. But they do release a bad smell when scared.

✗ marmorated—a color pattern that mixes white and brown and looks like a marble

WREAKING HAVOC

Stinkbugs and bedbugs are "true bugs." True bugs have a body part called a proboscis. A proboscis is a strawlike tube used to suck up food instead of chewing with jaws and teeth. The stinkbug uses its proboscis to suck juices from fruits and vegetables. Stinkbugs cause millions of dollars in damage to fruit trees and vegetables each year.

ARMIES OF ANTS

Have you ever watched ants crawling across your kitchen counter and wondered where they were going? They may have been **forager** ants. Forager ants are a type of worker ant. Workers are one of the three kinds of ants that live in a colony: the queen, workers, and males. Foragers leave a chemical smell behind that other ants in the colony can follow to find food. This is how an ant infestation begins.

• Worker pharaoh ants care for a queen in their colony.

Invaders Fact

Pharaoh ants can cause big problems by invading hospitals. A pharaoh ant infestation in a hospital is dangerous because the ants can carry many diseases. They may crawl into open wounds or the mouths of sleeping patients.

There are more than 12,000 recorded species of ants, but only a few are known to invade homes. These include the odorous house ant, pharaoh ant, and Argentine ant. Ant infestations are very difficult to control. The invading colony must be found and destroyed. However, the colony is usually located outside of the infested building. Ants are the number one reason people call exterminators for help.

⚠

TEENY TINY PESTS

Odorous ants, which are black, and pharaoh ants, which are yellow or brown, are very tiny. These ants love to eat sweet foods such as cookies and sugary snacks. They often make their colonies inside house walls, under carpets, or near hot water pipes.

✕ **forager**—a type of worker ant that leaves the colony to search for food

● Bedbugs feed on human blood every five to 10 days.

BEDBUG

Location: anywhere humans live

Why a problem? feed on human blood, causing itchy bumps and rashes

Key points:

- ☐ have fed on humans since ancient times
- ☐ came to North America with first European settlers
- ☐ almost impossible to get rid of without an exterminator

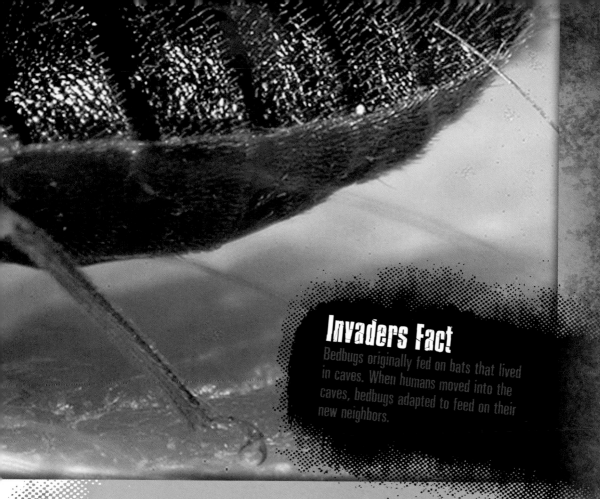

Invaders Fact

Bedbugs originally fed on bats that lived in caves. When humans moved into the caves, bedbugs adapted to feed on their new neighbors.

BEDBUGS DO BITE!

Bedbugs are tiny bloodsuckers that usually live in bedrooms. They use a proboscis to suck blood from sleeping humans. Bedbug bites cause itchy red bumps, similar to the bumps left behind by mosquito bites. Most people don't notice bedbugs in their homes until they have an infestation. Bedbugs are one of the most difficult insect invaders to get rid of.

CHAPTER THREE
FOLLOW THE CLUES

Knowing as much as you can about common insect invaders is the first step in preventing an infestation. But what do you do when you actually see one of these bugs in your house? Don't panic! First, become an insect detective. Looking for clues will help you determine if you really have an insect infestation and what you can do about it.

Ants and stinkbugs are among the easiest invaders to detect because they are usually more visible. You will know that you have a stinkbug infestation because you will see them everywhere in your house. Seeing one or two ants in your kitchen may be nothing to worry about. But if you spot a swarm of ants around a water or food supply, you might have an infestation.

A group of ants inside an infested building may be found near a food or water source.

ANT PLAN

If you have an ant infestation, you will probably need to hire an exterminator. Ant infestations often need to be stopped in different ways. Once the ant species has been identified, the exterminator will develop a plan. This plan will provide steps for locating and destroying the ant colony. The exterminator may also suggest ways to keep ants from entering your house in the future. The exterminator may have to use **pesticides** to kill the ants in the colony.

✕**pesticide**—poisonous chemical used to kill insects, rats, and fungi that can damage plants

17

NIGHTTIME NINJAS

Cockroaches sneak around your house at night—ninja style. These insects are **nocturnal**. Cockroaches also don't like light, so they hide in dark spaces. They have a waxy **exoskeleton**, which enables them to squeeze into a crack as thin as a credit card. While you're sleeping, they slip out of their hiding places in search of water and food.

SPOTTING THE SNEAKS

If cockroaches are so sneaky, how will you know if you have an invasion before it's too late? Here are some clues. Cockroaches always leave poop behind them. Their poop looks like black pepper. If you have a large infestation, there may be a strong, musty smell in your home. You may also find empty cockroach egg cases on kitchen shelves or behind appliances. These egg cases are shaped like tiny, brown cylinders. If you flip a light on at night and see cockroaches skittering back to their hiding places, you will also know you have a cockroach problem. And if you see a cockroach during the day, that probably means you have a huge infestation!

✖ **nocturnal**—an animal that is active at night and rests during the day

✖ **exoskeleton**—the hard outer shell of an insect; the exoskeleton covers and protects the insect

● Cockroaches prefer to live together in groups.

Invaders Fact

Cockroaches have amazing survival skills in the water. They can swim and hold their breath for up to 40 minutes.

BEASTLY BEDBUGS

Bedbugs are even sneakier than cockroaches. During the day, they hide in places such as the tiny cracks along mattress seams or inside the screw holes that hold a bed together. Bedbugs can be difficult to identify, but there are clues. Check along your bed's mattress and box spring, behind your headboard, and under couch cushions. Look for dark spots. These spots are dried bedbug poop. You may also see the leftover skins of bedbugs that have **molted**. A final clue is red smears. These smears come from the blood of crushed bedbugs.

Invaders Fact

Adult bedbugs can live as long as one year without eating.

✖ **molt**—to shed fur, feathers, or an outer layer of skin; after molting, a new covering grows

• Look under couch cushions for leftover bedbug skins.

⚠️
BEDBUG SNIFFING DOGS TO THE RESCUE

You've probably heard about dogs that are trained to sniff out bombs and drugs, but what about bedbugs? Dogs are trained to search for infestations in some places known to have bedbug problems. When these dogs smell bedbugs, they sit down. The specially trained dogs have been hired to work in apartment buildings, offices, hotels, and schools. They have found bedbugs not only under mattresses, but also in clock radios and behind wallpaper!

CHAPTER FOUR

FIGHTING BACK

BATTLING ANTS AND COCKROACHES

Once you discover a problem with ants and cockroaches, the first thing to do is block access to their food, water, and shelter. You can do this by filling in any cracks or crevices that the insects might be using to get into your house. Next, store food in airtight containers. Ants and cockroaches need fresh water. Try to identify and block all sources of water that they might be using, such as leaky faucets. But even all these steps may not solve your infestation problem.

You may have to use baits to get rid of some ant or cockroach infestations. Baits contain poison mixed with food. Cockroaches eat the poisoned food, and the poison slowly kills them. Ants eat the poisoned food and go back to the colony. They throw up their food to share with the other ants, including the queen. If the queen eats the poison and dies, the colony may eventually collapse.

Invaders Fact

Watch out for ants in the summer. In this season, many ants grow wings. Some fly off in search of a good location to start a new colony with a new queen.

● Argentine ants take poisoned food from a bait.

23

FIGHTING BEDBUGS

If you discover bedbugs, the first thing to do is vacuum around your bed and under the mattress. Then wash and dry all of your sheets, blankets, and pillowcases on high heat. But most bedbug infestations require a professional exterminator.

Bedbugs cannot survive at extremely high or low temperatures. The exterminator will use steaming, spot-freezing, or portable heaters to kill all the bedbugs and their eggs. Exterminators use handheld devices for steaming and spot-freezing. Portable heaters are placed in the infested buildings and will heat rooms to 130 degrees Fahrenheit (54 degrees Celsius).

FIGHTING STINKBUGS

One of the best ways to prevent or fight a stinkbug infestation is to seal any openings you have in your home. The good news is that stinkbugs will not lay eggs in your house. During the cold winter months, they enter a type of hibernation called **diapause**. In the spring, they will leave your house to lay their eggs.

×diapause—a period of time when an insect doesn't grow or develop and its body functions slow down

● An exterminator uses a handheld device to kill bedbugs.

CHAPTER FIVE
LIVING TOGETHER

During the 1950s bedbugs nearly became extinct in the United States because of the powerful pesticides used on them. Since then, many of these pesticides have been banned because they may damage the environment and cause sickness in animals and people. This has led to an increase in bedbug and other insect populations. People are now looking for safer ways to prevent and control insect infestations.

Baits made from a mixture of boric acid and sugar are one new method used to control ants and cockroaches. Insect invaders are attracted to the sugar and walk through the deadly boric acid. They carry the acid back to their nest or colony, where it kills any insects that eat it. This method is considered a safer choice because boric acid is not as dangerous to humans or the environment as some other substances.

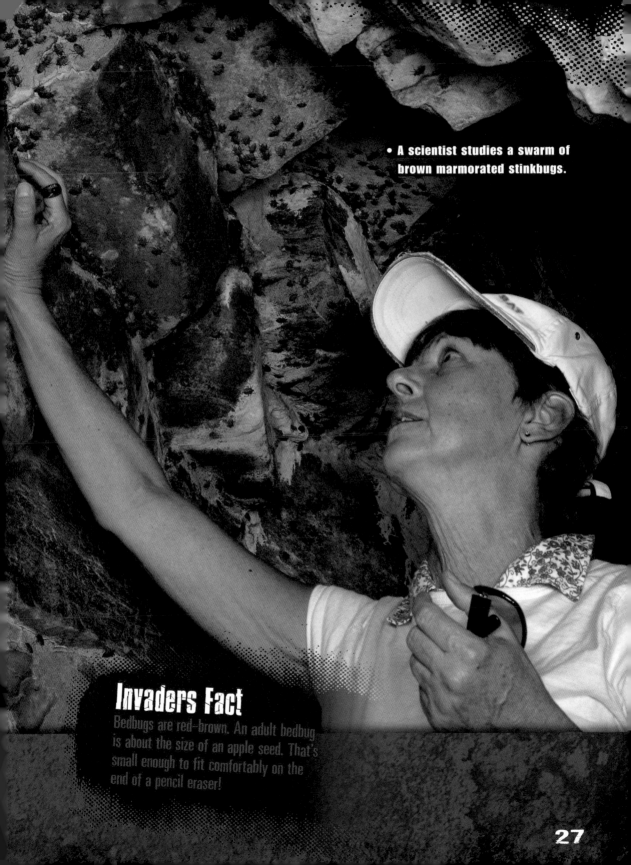

• A scientist studies a swarm of
brown marmorated stinkbugs.

Invaders Fact

Bedbugs are red-brown. An adult bedbug
is about the size of an apple seed. That's
small enough to fit comfortably on the
end of a pencil eraser!

• Ant workers carry eggs to safety after a disturbance in their colony.

BALANCING ACT

Insects play an important role in every environment they are a part of. Ants and cockroaches living in the wild feed on decaying wood, leaves, and animals. They add nutrients to the soil and make it better for growing plants. Insects also provide food for other animals. We may want to wipe out insect species that infest our homes, but this would harm the environment.

Insect invaders adapted by using humans to find food, water, and shelter. People have managed to live with infestations for hundreds of years. Humans will continue to adapt by learning new ways to prevent and manage insect infestations.

GLOSSARY

adapt (uh-DAPT)—to change to fit into a new or different environment

diapause (DY-uh-pawz)—a period of time in the life cycle of insects when their body functions slow down.

exoskeleton (ek-soh-SKE-luh-tuhn)—the hard outer shell of an insect; the exoskeleton covers and protects the insect.

exterminator (ik-STUHR-muh-nay-tuhr)—a person who rids places of unwanted pests for a living

forager (FOR-ij-ur)—an animal that looks for food

fossil (FAH-suhl)—the remains or traces of plants and animals that are preserved as rock

infestation (in-fes-TAY-shun)—a group of pests that can cause damage or harm

marmorated (MAR-muh-ray-tid)—in a marble-like pattern; white and brown mixed together

molt (mohlt)—shedding fur, feathers, or an outer layer of skin; after molting, a new covering grows

nocturnal (nok-TUR-nuhl)—active at night and resting during the day

pesticide (PES-teh-side)—poisonous chemical used to kill insects, rats, and fungi that can damage plants

species (SPEE-seez)—a group of plants or animals that share common characteristics

READ MORE

Claybourne, Anna. *A Colony of Ants, and Other Insect Groups.* Chicago: Heinemann Library, 2013.

Field, Jon Eben. *Scurrying Cockroaches* (Creepy Crawlies). New York: Crabtree Pub., 2011.

Gleason, Carrie. *Feasting Bedbugs, Mites, and Ticks* (Creepy Crawlies). New York: Crabtree Pub., 2011.

INTERNET SITES

FactHound offers a safe, fun way to find Internet sites related to this book. All of the sites on FactHound have been researched by our staff.

Here's all you do:

Visit *www.facthound.com*

Type in this code: 9781476501390

 Check out projects, games and lots more at
www.capstonekids.com

INDEX